THE TRUTH

ABOUT

AMERICAN ECONOMICS

By
Michael Vilkin
and
Michael A. George

MAG Publishing
1120 Ave. of the Americas
Suite 1061
New York, NY 10036

Library of Congress Catalog Card Number: 97-94241

ISBN 1-57502-573-6

Printed in the USA by

MORRIS PUBLISHING

3212 East Highway 30 • Kearney, NE 68847 • 1-800-650-7888

" The Truth About American Economics written by Michael A. George and Michael Vilkin is a well-planned and in-depth work that proffers your richly detailed survey of the intricate composition of American economics.

Arranged in a logical format, your treatise explores a host of related topics. You discuss the role of welfare within a democratic system, examine the complexities surrounding social security, explore the implications of having more than two dominant political parties, investigate the methodology behind a free-market system, and analyze the correlation between productivity and wages. In framing this guide with clear language, they render uncomplicated access to the core of their theories.

Their intricate design, keen attention to detail, extensive knowledge of their material, and thorough scope contribute to the informative nature of this chronicle."

Elizabeth H. House
Managing Director
Dorrance Publishing

Here's just some of what you'll learn in this remarkable new book!

First learn what this book will teach you:

How will you benefit from a health care reform plan in this book which is better the Clinton plan without unnecessary red tape ?

How will the solutions in this book benefit you ?

How to get a better understanding about economics ?

How you can get economic and political empowerment ?

How will you benefit from the information in this book on starting your own business ?

This book is a valuable resource guide for anyone who wants to know about The Truth About American Economics.

Michael A. George Publishing

I DEDICATE THIS BOOK TO:

My friends, Sonia James and Lenny Mathews, for their love and thoughfulness:

My family and relatives.

Special recognition to Michael Vilkin for giving me my first break and **C. A. Richards** for typing

this manuscript.

Trusting you will enjoy reading these lines and that this book will empower and inspire you, I love you all.

THE POWER IS IN YOUR HANDS

Power is something that we should take for granted.

So many people were denied equal rights years ago.

So many people gave up their lives so that we can have power.

As a young child, my mother told me about Dr. Martin Luther King, Jr., Malcolm X, John F. Kennedy, Robert F. Kennedy and etc.

These indiviuals had power and they were the messiahs.

These hands which once picked cotton will now pick an elected offical.

The Power Is In Yours Hands.

These hands which build this land, will now pull a dollar bill out of their wallets to make a purchase.

The Power Is In Your Hands.

As a diverse group of people, we must fight together for economic and social justice.

We are all God's children.

Power to the People !

Michael A. George

TABLE OF CONTENTS

Page

CHAPTER

1

PREFACE

Every day we are bombarded with economic problems. Welfare, unemployment, stagnating wages, cheap imports, robots, education, poor and hungry, savings, investments, Social Security, national debt, deficit spending, minimum wages, retirement.... How to make sense of it?

Most Americans are concerned about standard of living. Standard of living can be defined as affordability of goods and services. Today they are not as affordable as it used to be.

What should be done to improve the economy? Let us take a look , what average American needs to be happy? A house, furniture, a car, food, clothing, child care. How can we make these things affordable? We have to produce more. We have to build more houses, more child care centers, more nursing homes and so on.

If we increase supply of real estate, prices of real estate will go down and everybody will be able to buy a cheap house. If you pay less for your house, you save more money for other things and your standard of living goes up.

There are millions of people unemployed and on welfare. Why don't we put them to work to build those houses?

This book explains why people are kept on welfare and unemployed, and what we can do about it.

CHAPTER

2

WHAT IS ECONOMICS ?

Economics is a social science that deals with problems. "The problems of economics arise out of the use of scare resources to satisfy human wants." The resources of the society not only consist of free gifts from mother nature like land, forests and minerals. The gifts also includes human resources both mental and physical. Other means to help production includes tools, machinery and buildings.

"Economists call such resources Factors Of Production because they are used to produce those things that people desire. The things produced are called commodities." Commodities are goods and services. Goods are tangible for example, cars and shoes. Services are intangible for example, haircuts and education. Any good has value because of the service it benefits to the owner.

The automobile offers a service which consists of things like transportation, mobility and status. Production is derived from the act of making goods and services. Consumption result from the act of using to satisfy wants.

"Scarcity implies a need to choose and choice implies costs because a decision to have more of one thing requires a decision to have less of something else. The problem of choice arises over and over again in economics." The earliest form of free-market economics depended on barter which were goods traded for other goods.

Money was a form of exchange that was used to replace barter in business transactions. For an example, you want to buy a dress from a department store. In order to have that dress legally, you have to pay for that dress with money. "In a market economy, the allocation of resources is the outcome of millions of independent decisions made by consumers and producers, all acting through markets."

The decision makers in economics depend on three groups-households, forms and central authorities who will decide on market transactions. The definition of a household is all people who live under one roof. A household consists of one or two parents with children and a household can also include a single adult person.

"The firm is defined to be the unit that makes decisions regarding the employment of factors of production and the production of goods and services. It buys the services of the factors of production from households and sells the goods and services that it produces to other firms, to households, and to central authorities." An example of a firm is General Motors. General Motors produces automobiles as a means of production and their automobiles serviced a need for the American economy by creating jobs and a made of transportation.

The central authorities, in all cases, are called the government. The government is defined as public agencies, government bodies and other organizations belonging to or under the direct control of government. This includes the state, local and federal governments. In the United States, the central authorities consists of the President, the Federal Reserve System, the Congress, the State legislature, the City Council, and regulatory bodies, the police force and all government bodies that exercise control over the behavior of firms and households.

A market is an area where buyers and sellers negotiate the exchange of a well-defined commodity. An example of such a market is the Fulton Fish Market in the financial district of New York City. This is a market where fresh fish is brought early in the morning and sold by the end of the day. Firms which sell their output of goods and services are called product markets. Households which sell the services of the factors of production that they control are called factor markets.

A free market economy is an economy where decisions of individual households and firms cause the influence over the allocation of resources. A closed market economy is the opposite of a free market economy where the major decisions about the allocation of resources were made by government and in which firms and household produce and consume only as they are ordered.

Mixed economies are decisions made by firms, households and the government. In a mixed economy, we must know the difference between the public and private sector. The private sector consists of decisions made by households and firms. The public sector consists of decisions made by government.

3

THE CIRCULAR

FLOW OF ECONOMICS

There are two sets of markets, the factors markets and the product markets where decisions of firms and households takes effect. The members of households needs commodities to feed, clothed, housed, entertained and secured. They also want to educate and beautify themselves. They are forced to make choices on what goods and services that they can afford in product markets. Households respond to product-market prices for every set of prices. Households will always make choices.

The factors of production are brought by firms. "The quantities demanded depend on the firms production decisions, which in turn depend on consumers demand." The demand for the factors will have an effect on the prices of labor, managerial skill, raw materials, buildings, machinery, use of capital, land and all other factors. The household are owners of factors must respond to factor prices and make decisions on where to offer their services. Their choices determine factor supplies and have and affect on factor prices. "Payments by firms to factor owners provide the owners of the factors with incomes." The households are recipients of the incomes. The members of the households want the commodities to keep them fed, clothed, housed and entertained. We have completed the circular Flow.

Factors services from households to firms and money flow in the form of income from firms to households. Goods and services in the form of consumption are sold through product markets. Real flow of goods and services from firms to households and the money flow consists of payments from household to firms.

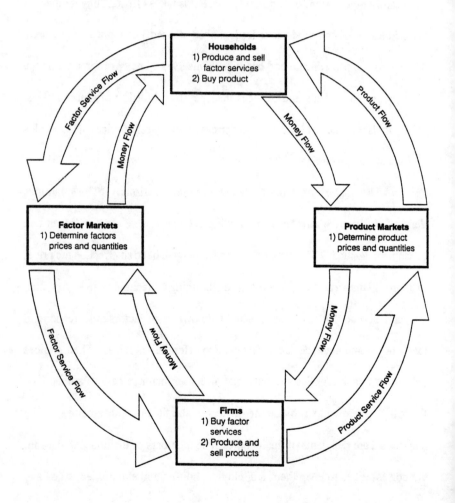

CHAPTER

4

WHAT IS MONEY?

Let us take a look at a dollar bill. What is it? You own something, it may be a pen, a notebook, a pound of chicken. You own a small piece of this country. The dollar bill is a certificate of ownership.

Should we increase minimum wage so that poor people get richer? If everybody gets twice more certificates of ownership of the same amount of wealth, nobody will get richer. We will create twice more shares of wealth, but not wealth.

We need full employment and as high productivity as possible. If robots are more productive than workers, workers must be replaced by robots. All in the name of higher productivity. What will do those replaced workers ? We will discuss it later.

The main function of money is it's function as a certificate of ownership of the wealth of a given country. The more wealth is produced in this country, the more value has the money.

When you have money, you have wealth. When you have no money, you are just broke. You will not have wealth when you are employed by someone else. You will have more wealth when you are self-employed. You will be rewarded with wealth after you worked hard building your business. The Book of Psalms in the Bible will tell you, "When you worked the land, the pasture will be fertiled with the fruits of your labor" Use this inspirational message to build your wealth and American Dream.

CHAPTER

5

PRODUCTIVITY AND WAGES

We know that wages in the USA are higher than the wages in Mexico. What does it mean? We can think about our economy as a big table. Producers bring their goods and services to the table, where they are exchanged.

We already know that a dollar is just a share of the wealth on our table. Wages in the USA are than Mexican wages not because we are paid a lot of dollars. We bring to our table a lot of chickens, and computers, and everything else.

We can print money and give everybody twice more dollars, but if we don't produce more chickens, the price of a chicken will be twice higher. It's not high wages. It's high productivity.

The same reasoning is true about Mexican table. Simply put, if they can not afford to buy a chicken, it's not because they are paid low wage.

It's because they don't produce enough chickens. The trick is to identify what we really need to produce. There are a few industries, which can employ welfare recipients. One of those industries is the construction industry.

By using welfare recipients, they will learn a new skill at a lower cost to business government.

Other industries will also benefit by using welfare recipients.

Empowerment Zones should be created to give tax breaks to business for putting welfare recipients to work.   Private sector investment in low income neighborhoods makes sense.

Welfare recipients will be more productive by giving them an incentive to work. We must show them that earning a paycheck is better than getting a welfare check.

CHAPTER

6

EXCHANGE RATES

We already know that money is shares of wealth or this country.

Now let us take a look at exchange rates.

Why we exchange one dollar for a few Mexican pesos? Why not one dollar for one peso?

Suppose we can buy one pound of chicken in the USA for one dollar. Suppose also that we can buy one pound of chicken in Mexico for one peso. The exchange rate is one dollar for one peso.

Can we export or import chickens? No. We exchange one share of American wealth for an equal share of Mexican wealth. No profit in either direction.

Suppose now, that the prices are one dollar and one peso, respectively, but exchange rate for one dollar is two pesos. Wow!

We can buy one pound of chicken in Mexico for one peso move it across the board and sell it for one dollar. That dollar we exchange for two pesos, and we are in a good business.

For the sake of simplicity, we didn't take to the account any expenses like transportation and tariffs, which is tax for import. But the idea is clear, money is only as good as it's buying power. In the future, when there is a free market and no tariffs, exchange rates will reflect exactly buying power of the money.

CHAPTER

7

PROFITABILITY

We already know that the most important function of money is it's function as a share of the wealth of a given country. We know also that exchange rates of money depend mostly on purchasing power of money.

Now let us take a look at the concepts of price and profit. Thousands of years ago people didn't know much about economic theories, but they did follow basic rules of the market. Even in a primitive moneyless economy, producers followed the rule of a profit.

Suppose, one day of work was needed to make a pair of shoes and one day of work was needed to make a piece of clothing. Suppose also, that a pair of shoes was exchanged for one chicken. A piece of clothing was exchanged for two chickens.

We can just imagine that producers did not really need any formulas to figure it out, that it was more profitable to produce clothing. Not shoes.

Today, we use money as medium of exchange but that simple formula of profitability did not really change. Today as thousands of years ago, producers are looking for opportunities to produce goods and services, which are more profitable to produce.

The prices on raw materials to produce goods must go down. The service sector must decrease the cost of charging people for a service. The cost of labor must be lowered in order for businesses to make a profit. This is a reason why so many American corporations go to third world nations to produce goods while workers in these countries earned slave wages. Take my advice, the next time when you buy clothing or a new pair of shoes, look at the label or the written inscription to find about Made In _____. The next time you may a purchase, look for Made in the USA label.

CHAPTER

8 PRICES IN A FREE MARKET

What producers are likely to do when they see that to produce clothing is more profitable than to produce shoes? Producers will increase production of more profitable clothing and decrease production of less profitable shoes.

When producers increase supply of clothing, the price of it will decrease. When producers decrease supply of shoes, the price of shoes will increase. Eventually, the prices of shoes and clothing will reach levels at which they are equally profitable to produce.

Prices are determined by supply and demand. Demand is amount of money consumers are willing to spend for a particular good of service at a particular price. If a price of a particular good or service goes down, demand for it goes up. This is so because at a lower price more people will be able to afford it.

For example, many people can not afford to buy new cars. If the prices of new cars were lower, more people would be able to afford them. As we see supply of goods and services in a free market depends on level of productivity. The problem is that we don't have an efficient free market.

One problem is that statistics of profitability are not readily available. Another problem is that there are many roadblocks on the way to start profitable business. The roadblock to building a profitable business is too many regulations. Too many regulations also lead to bureaucracy. Small businesses creates new jobs.

Government is not in business of creating jobs. Businesses creates jobs and government must lower the tax burdens on small businesses to create jobs. Small business will pass on the costs of paying higher taxes to consumers in terms of higher prices. We need deregulation. Deregulation will bring in competition with businesses for lower prices. Lower prices means more profits.

CHAPTER

9

PRODUCTIVITY OF A WORKER

VERSUS

PRODUCTIVITY OF A SYSTEM

Suppose, there is family of ten people, living on a farm. They produce ten pounds of bread daily and they are hungry. There is a second family of ten people, and they produce twenty pounds of bread daily. They work as hard as the first family and, they know the farm work better.

There is a third family of ten people. They produce ten pounds of apples, and they exchange ten pounds. They produce in terms of bread, thirty pounds of it.

Suppose now that the neighborhood went to the dogs, and every family needs a watchman. One member of each family becomes a watchman with the understanding that he will receive an equal portion of the family's output.

Suppose now that watchmen of the first and the second families organized an International Brotherhood of Watch men and demanded equal wages with the third watchman. The reason is as simple as a straight line in a sand and a watchman is a watchman. Productivity of the trade group is the same and wages must be the same. Three pounds of bread. Should they get it?

Wages depend on productivity of an economic system. A doorman in my apartment building has the same productivity as a doorman in Mexico.

CHAPTER

10   CHEAP LABOR

Suppose now that the third family decided to hire the watchman for the first family and pay him all the wages of the third family. The watchman from the first family will be happy. True, one point five pounds of bread is not as food as tree pounds, but much better than one pound he was paid in the first family.

Now let us take a look what is happening here. The watchman from the first family will do the same job for half wages. Is is good for the third family? Yes, it is. He brings something to the table, but takes from the table only half of the wages. More is left on the table for the third family.

What is happening when American companies close production plants here and move to low wage countries? The watchman will work for half wages.

Let us take look at an American economy as a big table. Producers bring their products to the table, where they are exchanged. Suppose, one producer of shoes moved his plant to Mexico. American workers were paid two chickens. Mexican workers are paid one chicken per hour. They are as productive as Americans. What happened here? How unproductive Mexicans instantly became as productive as Americans?

The answer is really simple. Productivity of manual workers, both Mexicans and Americans are the same, if they are given the same machinery.

American workers are more productive on more productive equipment and machinery. I don't think that American bricklayer is more productive than the Mexican bricklayer.

What happens when a Mexican is hired instead of an American to produce shoes? He will produce the same shoes for half the wages. He will bring to the American table the same shoes and exchange them for one chicken instead of two. If we were one family, we would say that is good. Shoes from the Mexican table are exchanged for one chicken from the American table.

We wouldn't like to give Mexicans more chickens. The chickens we give them, the less will be left on our table and more children will go hungry.

American worker was replaced for a good reason, to give him an opportunity to get another job. No jobs out there? There are millions of jobs we have to create. Just take a look what we can't afford. Let us build those houses and day care centers, and one hundred and one things we can't afford. We can't afford houses, day care for children, dance and music lessons and so on, and so on, and so....

We need to increase the supply of real estate.

CHAPTER

11

STANDARD OF LIVING

OF THE NATION

Standard of living may be defined as affordability of goods and services produced by the economic system. Those goods and services are houses for everybody, furniture, chickens in every pot and so on. What is amazing and amusing, is that liberals say that you need college education to have a house and everything in the house. Not true. Houses were built and chickens were raised thousands of years ago. You don't need any high technology to build houses for everybody.

By now everybody should understand that the more we bring to the table the higher standard of living of the nation. All goods and services produced by the economy are Gross National Product. The higher GNP the higher standard of living should be. When we replace workers by more productive robots, we increase GNP. When we exchange some goods from our table for cheap goods from Mexico, we increase amount of goods on our table. Both ways, we increase standard of living of the nation. But not standard of living of SOME workers.

For example, if Mexican workers produce shoes and sell them cheaper in USA, American producers of shoes will be hurt. Their profits will be lower but lower prices for shoes are very good for the rest of USA.

Cheap imports increase standard of living in USA. The best way to

18

increase standard of living in this country is to reduce unemployment down to no more than one or two percent. Education? Forget it. Now we need brick layers. Why bricks? Read on. We can not afford to buy houses, to pay for child care, for sport activities, for dancing lessons, for ... anything. Our children wonder on the streets. The solution is really simple. Let us define the problem and after that look for the solution. Price of everything depends on supply and demand. Increase the supply of anything, and the price of it will go down. What is the most expensive thing in the economy? We don't realize that most money is spent on real estate. Whatever business you are in, a big expense item is real estate. The costs are passed on to the consumer and that is why our children wonder on the streets. It's not that music and dance lessons are expensive. In final analysis, we pay for the real estate. Bring the price of real estate down, and prices of everything will go down. Can we increase supply of the real estate? Easy. Just lay bricks. Retirement for Boomers? Just lay bricks. If every Boomer has a dirt-cheap house, part of our retirement worries are gone. The goal is clear. How to reach it? How to protect agricultural land from real estate development? Where to build new real estate? How to overcome resistance of the real estate magnates, who will fight us tooth and nail?

Government should create special zones for the real estate development where R.E. Developers would be free from taxes. Millions of jobs will be created in the construction industry.

CHAPTER

12   SOCIAL SECURITY

Every day we hear that social security is in trouble and we need to save money to fund the retirement. The truth is that we don't need to save money. Standard of living of retirees will depend on prices of food, clothing and rent. The biggest item is rent. If a person owns a house or an apartment, he or she is much more secure financially than those who will depend on market to rent an apartment.

It will be, probably, better to own an apartment and to have $500 a month Social Security check than to rent an apartment and to have $1000 a month check. If rent prices go up, millions of people will be forced to make a choice between food and shelter. Millions of old people may become homeless.

What should we do to protect Baby boomer generation from becoming a Homeless generation? Should we save money to protect ourselves? Should we increase Social Security taxes? No, no, no! If the rent prices go up sharply, no money in the world will protect people. Both our savings and Social Security fund will disappear in no time at all.

We need to give millions of people vocational training to build houses. If millions of people start to build houses, supply of houses will go down and almost everybody will own a house or an apartment.

CHAPTER

13 WELFARE POLITICS

People need a college education to build houses. Some vocational training would be enough. Why don't we give millions of people vocational training to build houses? Now all the talk about welfare is that they need education. They need child care that they can not afford. Why they can not afford child care? High prices.

Why prices are high? Supply is low. Can increase supply of child care? Easy. Just put people to work to build those child care centers. Why Democrats do not want to do it? The problem is that big real estate owners are Democrats. For me, it's easy to propose to build houses and drive rent prices and child care prices down.

Real estate owners are not interested to drive rent prices lower. Lower prices mean lower profits. This is the reason why Democrats are talking about education and they don't talk about jobs for ordinary people.

The Democratic Party needs millions of disadvantaged people to vote for them. These poor people are forced to stay on welfare and vote for rich Democrats. Fortunately, some black leaders started to understand the situation. They are talking about a third party.

By having a third party, People will have a voice. People will be seen and heard and people will be treated with respect. Politicians will not take votes for granted. When you vote in elections, you will show real power. Real power was something that Dr. Martin Luther King, Jr. and Malcolm X had to influence masses of people to march and protest. I challenge all people to stand up and fight. People should invest their money in their communities by buying real estate and people should build buildings and houses on those properties.

CHAPTER 14

THE RECESSION AFFECTED
SO MANY PEOPLE

As co-author of this book and a successful African-American male, I will write about my own personal experience dealing with the recession. I had a lot of personal ambition. I landed my first real job with New York Newsday and I started this job a few weeks before my college graduation in January 1988. This job came with fringe benefits like health insurance, profit sharing, automobile mileage and cash expenses reimbursement.

I enjoyed this job because I had worked toward this type of career during my college days. Everyone had hopes and dreams like myself. I was successful in terms of reaching my lifetime goal of graduating from college and I was the first person in my family to graduate with two college degrees. Before the Spring of 1992, the recession had a rumbling effect on the economy of the United States and the New York City metropolitan area. Large retail establishments, large corporations and some airlines filed for Chapter 11 bankruptcy.

When advertising revenues were low, a newspaper can not meet the costs of doing business. Cuts had to be made and the ax was ready to fall. I was given a severance package to read from the human resource manager in April 1992. After careful consideration, I decided to go for early retirement after working four and half years for New York Newsday.

The Summer of 1992 was a rough summer for me in terms of being laid-off for the first time. I was depressed as I visited the unemployment office. While I was standing on the unemployment line, I noticed other people on the line were middle management personnel. I felt even more depressed because those individuals had large mounting bills to pay. Layoffs affected the middle class more than the poor. The middle class were sinking deeper into poverty. I heard of news reports about people committing suicide due to being laid off from a job and they can no longer provide for their families.

I got over my depression by talking to other people at job counseling sessions. At these sessions, I met middle aged people who were laid off from their jobs. These counseling sessions helped me boost my self-esteem as a person. I sent out letters and resumes in order to request a job interview. I had received several rejection letters for being over-qualified and under-qualified for jobs. I applied to work at an insurance company selling life insurance for the first time. I was fired for not making my sales quota during a two month period. In the Summer of 1993, I volunteered my time to work for a mayoral re-election campaign in New York City and I was doing community service work in poor communities. I was given more respect from people due to being a volunteer. I started another job selling life insurance for another insurance company. I held this job for eight months because I wasn't making enough money in order to pay my bills at home. I accomplished one thing by earning the rookie of the month plaque for selling the most insurance policies for April 1994.

I was working as a supervisor for a private security company. This job only lasted for eight months and I was discharged from my duties. I was unemployed again and I decided to look for another job. I had received several rejection letters from perspective employers and I became very depressed during my job search. I thought that the reason for not being hired was due to my employment history.

The real reason for not being hired was based on racial discrimination. I was well-educated and I spoke with such great articulation. I was always well dressed for job interviews. A lot of African-American males went through the same experience that I had gone through. The unemployment rate among African American males is the highest among other ethnic groups' unemployment rate in this country. America does have a very serious race problem.

Everyday is a day of atonement for me and I am grateful to God for helping me get over so many obstacles in my life. Despite the problems that I had in the past, I always made my life secondary to others who needed my help first. I retained my honesty and integrity as a person who lived in the United States for all of my life. Thousands of young people graduating out of college cannot find jobs because they do not have access to a crowded job market.

Government can create free market labor by creating jobs. We can train people for jobs in road and highway construction. The government can create jobs and the government can provide funds for highway construction projects. The infrastructure is crumbling in our nation's cities. Free market labor can solve the problem of unemployment in this country.

CHAPTER

15   ECONOMIC OPPORTUNITIES

Some politicians are in favor of the private sector creating jobs but there is one problem. During the recession, the private sector had cut so many jobs. For example in 1995, Chase Manhattan Bank and Chemical Bank merged and 12,000 employees were laid off. In 1970, the average length of employment at one company is ten years. In 1990, the average of employment is there years and six months. Job security is no longer the answer for long-term employment.

Many job seekers include highly trained professionals, office and blue collar workers. There are job training programs for dislocated workers through the federal government. Grants from the job training programs are distributed through the states, for the training programs to be administrated by local agencies. The federal government assumes that dislocated workers do not need classroom training to get jobs. Dislocated workers will need only readjustment training or job counseling. How true that is depends largely on the job market and the local economy.

Some people are frustrated when they worked for someone. The reasons for their frustrations are the following: The glass ceiling, lack of opportunities, psychological burnout and not making enough money.

Entrepreneurship is an excellent option for those seeking to be self-employed.

Self-employment can be gained through the following: Direct marketing, you can do part-time and this can be turned into a business.

To learn more about entrepreneurship, you may take a course at a college or university. As an entrepreneur, you may learn about management, fiancé, marketing and legal matters. You will have to write a business plan, you must include the following information: The type of business, location of the business, five year sales projections, the type of equipment for the business and income tax returns from the last three years.

To learn more about writing a business plan, you may contact the Small Business Development Center and the Service Corps of Retired Executives (SCORE).

The Urban Business Assistance Corporation (UBAC) provides consulting services to aspiring entrepreneurs as well as existing business owners. The UBAC can help you develop a Business Plan, Marketing Strategies, Organizational Analysis, Loan Proposals and Feasibility Studies.

The Urban Business Assistance Corporation is privately funded, not for profit organization affiliated with the New York University Leonard N. Stern School of Business.

UBAC was founded in 1969 to provide technical assistance to minority owned businesses in the New York metropolitan area.

The background of each UBAC participants are as diverse as their business interests. UBAC has assisted a variety of retail, manufacturing and service businesses in developing their management skill. Through the unique combination of low-cost classes and consulting services, UBAC continues to provide vital resources to many of New York's minority business owners. For more information, you may contact the New York University Leonard N. Stern School of Business.

Self-employment can also lead to new job creation and you don't have to worry about losing your job. Having a good reputation is very important in business. People not only buy your product, they also buy your personality. I learned in the insurance business that people will buy from you as long as they can trust you. Good service is very important in business because your reputation relies on it. Affirmative Action had improved the economic development of many African-Americans. A lot of African-Americans don't realized that Affirmative Action was created by Conservatives.

For the first time, African-Americans were given an equal footing in the workplace and in terms of getting government contracts. African-Americans were denied loans in order to start a business and this reason was due to redlining. In my opinion, redlining is defined as not permitting to loan out money to applicants living in low income areas.

This practice of relining had been going on for several years by white owned banks. Most African-American deposited their money in white owned banks. Congress passed the Community Reinvestment Act (CRA). This act forced financial institutions to loan out money to minority communities. Financial Institutions are grade on a system based on the percentage of money being loaned out to the minority community. The CRA is also enforced by the banking department in each state.

Financial Institutions are being pressured to stop redlining to the minority community. If you have any questions about The Community Reinvestment Act, please contact any financial institution or the State Banking Department.

In the Black community, African-Americans do not control the local economy. The grocery stores, fruit stands, supermarkets, pharmacies and etc. are owned by other ethnic groups. Those businesses in the black community do not hire African-Americans as employees, meanwhile, African-Americans support these businesses. We must support the black owned businesses as a way to show our clout.

People had complained about problems in their communities. Organizing a peaceful protest is one way to solve a problem but sometimes, protests can lead into violence. For example, urban riots in the 1960's and the Watts riots in Los Angeles in 1992. Riots destroys neighborhoods and the federal government neglected rebuilding these neighborhoods.

Economics is affected by politics and a lot of people don't know how to play politics. One way of playing politics is to become involve in a community based organization. For an example, the community based organizations consists of Block Associations, The NAACP, National Urban League, Political Party Club, the Rotary Club and etc. Members of these community-based organizations can also attend police precient community council meetings in your city.

Citizens can complained about the quality of life issues in their communities. The police will respond to the quality of life issues based among numerous complaints. The Community Boards also played a valuable role in getting financial resources to the communities.

The community board consists of working professionals, entrepreneurs and community activists. The community board votes on issues which affects the community. The District Manager of the Community Board chaired the meeting. The community board meets once a month and the public is invited to attend the meetings. You may also attend community board committee meetings. I will explained about one in detail from my personal experience.

I attended the Economic Development Committee meeting. This meeting was chaired by a board member and members of the committee consists of community residents.

This committee has access to state and federal programs in reference to the economic development of the community. Money had been allocated from government budgets in the form of government grants for small businesses in the community. This money can be used for business improvements and business start-ups. Residents should get involve with this committee so that they can get access to these funds.

The Community Board has power and influence in local politics. Politicians are not only held accountable by the voters. They are also held accountable by the community boards, please contact the local community board in your neighborhood.

Voting in local elections is very important as you exercise your right to vote. Politicians are very concerned about their jobs on election day. You may vote for a political who will work for you.

Venture capital is one way which African-American can get financing for their business. Specialized Small Business Investment Corporation is an example of venture capital. Minority Enterprise Small Business Investment Corporation is an example of venture capital. The primary sources of funding for SSBICs consists of the following: institutional investors (pension funds), insurance companies and private partnerships. Private corporations are given tax incentives by making funds available to finance minority businesses.

The Small Business Investment corporation (SBIC) program was created in 1959 due to a Federal Reserve Board report which showed a lack of equity financing for pioneering and manufacturing small business in the start-up and growth phases. Twenty years after the start of MESBICs, they had assisted African-American, Hispanic, Asian-American and Native American business owners. MESBICs were changed into SSBICs by Congress.

SSBICs were created by the Nixon Administration's Black Capital program. American politicians and corporate executives must understand that they can make money in the minority community. A relationship must be established between government, public and private investors and the minority small businessperson.

Business incubators can serve as a great resource for minorities and women to obtain financing for their business. Business incubators can be appealing because they provide flexible leases, administrative services, shared office equipment and they allow new and established firms to operate under one roof.

Tenants will have access to experts such as accountants, lawyers, sales reps and management consultants who work pro bono. Business incubators are financed by the following sources: government and non profit organizations, investment groups, and real estate development firms. These incubators are created for the empowerment of minorities and women. For more information, you may contact the nearest business incubator in your are:

New York
Latimer Woods Economic Development Association
395 Flatbush Avenue
Brooklyn, NY 11201
(718) 237-2585

For more information on starting your own business or improving your business, please contact the following:

The Caribbean American Chamber of Commerce and Industry, Inc.
(718) 834-4544

Unlimited Creative Enterprises Information and Referral Services
(718) 638-9675

National Minority Business Council, Inc.
(212) 573-2362

Queens County Overal Economic Development Corporation
(781) 262-8383

Minority & Women Business Loans
(718) 636-6924

Bootstrap Business-Newsletter
(215) 844-7655

CHAPTER

16 ADVOCATES FOR POVERTY

There are thousands of non-profit organizations who stated that their mission is to help poor and hungry. They survive on private donations and government grants. We already know that soup kitchens are not the answer. Charitable organizations do more harm than good. The problem is that contributions to charity are tax deductible. At first glance, it seems that this should be this way. The math of charity is dishwashing. People donate old junk to charities and for every dollar donated, they get ten dollars of tax deductions. If you have and old car which you can sell for one hundred dollars, you may donate it to charity. It is a good way to reduce your taxes. Old furniture and paintings are even a better way to reduce taxes. Everything old and worthless will do the trick. Millions of dollars escape the IRS every year. What is good? The only thing is that those miserable advocates help keep themselves employed. Non-profit organization executives draw fat salaries and ride on the back of the public. It's time to make donations to these parasites not tax deductible. Advocates for the poor demand more money for education. This is a stated goal. The reality is that money is being looted.

There are dozens of technical schools in New York City. For example, they teach you typing. After the school year, you can't find a job because you don't have experience. You can't type 50 words a minute. You stay on welfare, while the school is getting it's share of loot. On paper, it was spent on education.

On practice, it was looted by the crooks. They are in business to make money and they are also in business not to educate you.

Government should not pay these fraudulent schools who stole taxpayers dollars. Actually, they should be closed. That's not simple and these schools are not just schools, they are schools owned by friendly people. At election time, these friends will make donations. They should pay back some of the looted money and they will provide money for political support. This is a dirty world of advocates for the poor and hungry.

If they really want to help poor and hungry, they should teach the poor real business skills. For example, there are millions of cars in New York City. These cars need maintenance. You have to change oil, filters and brakes once in a while. You have to take good care of your car to prevent a major problem from developing. This is very much like preventive care to avoid emergency room. This preventative care for the car is not exactly for a rocket scientist to understand. One year of school would do the trick. Is there a market for it? Yes, there is a huge market. Thousands of owners don't go to a shop for certain type of service. For example, to take apart a carburetor and clean it costs two hundred dollars. Who wants to pay so much money until the car is dead? Not so many people. Why should we pay $45 per hour for such maintenance work? Who is fixing prices in this supposedly free market?

We all know that there are many people who say that welfare recipients are lazy. Let us give unemployed people an opportunity to do this job for $15 per hour. We will pay to the owner of the shop $30 per hour. The biggest problem is not that people don't have skills. The problem for this is to get a market share of this automobile maintenance market. A lot of work in automobile maintenance is not done because of prohibitive price or the work. For better or worse, welfare reform is just around the corner and we are going to see if people are really lazy. We should hope that fraudulent schools will be closed. Money should be spent on real education, therefore, preparing for real jobs.

Welfare and unemployment are the causes of crime. Those who work are not troublemakers. We have no choice but to organize our economy that way, everybody has an opportunity to work. Are you a rocket scientist or a maintenance worker? You must work and contribute something to the society.

There are advocates for prison inmates. They say prisons are under funded. Let us take a look at that money. It costs twenty thousand dollars! A small apartment in Forest Hills, New York plus food will cost around ten thousand dollars a year for two people. $10,000 for two against $20,000 for one. An apartment in Forest Hills, New York is not exactly like a prison cell. Isn't there a problem with money management? Wouldn't it be cheaper to bring all those inmates to the Forest Hills apartments, and feed them with healthy food? We would save money on jails. This money is not spent on inmates and this money is being looted. Too many people make a living from the corrections system. New prisons have been constructed in New York State. Average price for a prison cell is more than 150 thousand dollars each. For $150,000, every inmate could have bought a big house near the same prison. There is not rational explanation to this looting of taxpayers money.

Some people say, public schools are being underfunded and not enough money to fund the public school system in New York City. Members of the

Board of Education spend money on expensive gifts for themselves. They organize conferences somewhere in exotic locations, there is no law and there is no order.

Public school teachers say that students don't like math because they are poor. The author of this book would go to the public school, who ever is worst in math, and he would teach them math and economics combined. They would start with the example of the fair price of a chicken in Italy and then, they would finish with calculating fair salaries for public school teachers. At that moment, all the public schools would be finished. Students would learn that the only difference between a good teacher and a bad teacher is that a good teacher would teach well for $20,000 a year. Is it any wonder that the author will not be given a chance to teach poor students so much math?

Now we can answer an interesting question. Why government is so inefficient but so many people want to increase the size of the government? Are they stupid or what? No, they are not stupid. They understand that government is exactly the place where they can suck money and life out of the economy. They will do it as long as they say that we need more money for the poor and hungry. As long as they say it, we believe them. We are stupid. We don't need money for the poor and hungry. We need to reinvent a free market, not government. We need to rediscover the island, everybody will be able to enter into the free labor market and contribute something to the society. We don't need more prison cells but we need more jobs. Only a free market society can create conditions where there are equal wages for equal work. Our poor and hungry folks will be no longer be poor nor hungry. Advocates for the poor and hungry will no longer exist. It is too bad for them.

CHAPTER

17   N.Y. STATE ECONOMY
vs. U.S.A. STATE ECONOMY

There is a new Republican world order out there. They promised us lower taxes and more jobs. We had voted the Democrats out and we had voted the Republicans in. Will they be better? We already know that lower taxes doesn't mean lower unemployment. Taxes are not bad. Looting of tax dollars is bad. Will Republicans loot less than Democrats. The name of the game is division of the big pie. Everybody wants a piece of the pie for their constituents. Constituents are those businesses which had contributed to the campaigns. In this money game, who cares about the average Joe? Who cares about this county? We are talking about distribution and redistribution of income.

In New York State, a Democratic governor was replaced by a Republican who promised lower taxes and more jobs as an economic stimulus. The truth is that there is not very much room for that on the state level. Suppose for a minute, a Republican delivered even more than we want and we produced a miracle. As a result, free market economy is enforced in New York State. Labor unions won't demand more money. Everybody makes as much money as he desires. The big gap between the third class population and the first class labor aristocrats exists no more.

There is a new automobile factory in Harlem where the former welfare recipients can make affordable cars at $10 per hour in wages. Other people can build affordable housing for the same wages. Workers can now afford to buy each other's products because wages are determined by a free market. There are equal wages for equal jobs. There will be no more welfare and no more unemployment. There will be low taxes. What would happen?

The "disadvantaged" and "less fortunate" from all over this country would arrive in New York State. This pure stupidity to suggest that lower taxes would revitalize the economy of New York State or any other state. Lower taxes don't create jobs. Lower taxes help steal jobs from other states where taxes are higher. If we give General Motors an incentive to pay no taxes for their new manufacturing plant in Harlem, General motors will steal jobs from Detroit. General Motors will produce one million cars in Harlem, but one million cars less in Detroit. New York jobs will not be created--jobs were stolen, replaced, removed or whatever. What will happen to those "disadvantaged people" who were laid off? They will move from Detroit to Harlem? Zero. The whole idea to "create" jobs is stupid. Suppose we train unemployed people to sell vegetables. The Koreans will be put out of business and they will go on welfare. Unemployed people learn to make better pizzas than the Italians, then the Italian pizza makers will go on welfare.

We should understand that we in N.Y. State, don't need to have the lowest taxes in the country so that everybody moves into New York City. There is already too much congestion and we don't need to move Detroit into Central

Park. We need to create jobs on a federal level and not to steal jobs from Detroit. There is only one way to do it. We must create free market labor on the federal level.

The idea of a free labor market is simple but we are going to see a lot of resistance form labor unions. Nobody wants to contribute more to the table of a free market economy. Everybody want to grab more from the table but this is not a way to improve the economy. Auto workers don't want to give anybody access to their protected area. They don't want lower prices for their cars which were manufactured in the automobile factories. Home builders feel the same. Nobody wants welfare recipients in their cars which were manufactured in the automobile factories. Home builders feel the same. Nobody wants welfare in their protected areas of the economy. As a result, we have a segment of population where there is no hope. All we need is a law which would allow an employer to pay off any union member, if there is someone willing to do the same job for half the wages. It will be a step in the right direction and there will be economic justice for all Americans living in this country.

CHAPTER

18   TAXES

We all know that taxes are bad. Government is bad because they tax us to death. When we have less money to spend, this is bad for the economy. We should cut taxes, the logic goes, we will have more money to spend, and it will be good for the economy. Is it correct? This logic is correct for the Italian economy. Just give me more money, take less taxes from me, and everything will be okay.

There is but a logic. When we are taxed, we have less money to spend. It is bad for the economy. Yes, correct. Money is never lost in the economy. Let us take a look at what happens with a dollar which was taxed out of your pocket. This dollar goes to the government. At this moment, there are two ways. The first way is to give this dollar to the crooks who deliver $150,000 prison cells. It costs $20,000 a year to educate inmates in prisons. They are not liberals, as we commonly refer to them, they are parasites.

We should notice that the dollar is still alive. From your pocket, it has been redistributed to their pocket. There is no difference to the economy what this dollar is being spent for. You will buy two hamburgers but someone will buy one more pizza. Your hamburger is not better than his Cappuccino. This redistribution is not bad for the economy but it is bad for you.

The second way, is to spend this dollar for something at market price. For example, public schools, hospitals and transportation; labor unions and market prices are not exactly compatible because tax dollars are looted here.

Suppose for a minute that our tax dollars are spent for necessary services at fair market prices. In this case, why are taxes bad? You would pay a public school teacher the same $20,000 a year income as you would pay for a teacher in a private school. Money would not be looted.

Taxes are not bad but looting tax dollars is very bad. Liberals are not stupid. We are.

CHAPTER

19   RUMOR CONTROL

The author of this book doesn't have any intention of becoming a leader of the third party. There are millions of scientists, engineers and college kids who may become part of the party. Economists who are not on a payroll of PIGs. You are very welcome to join the new party. Tax lawyers and accountants who want to simplify the tax codes. Everybody who believes that the future belongs to science, high technology, free labor market and social security for all members of society. You are very welcome to join. Pass this book to your friends and organize the party from the bottom. We don't have to belong to the traditional two party system. As a member of a third political party, you will be able to stand proud against the Democrats and the Republicans. You can tell Congress that doing politics as usual will no longer exist. We need to have more members of the third political party to hold public office. In my opinion, the third party really represent the views of the American people. This third party will bring change to the present political landscape. It's time for Real change.

CHAPTER

20   WE NEED A THIRD PARTY

This country needs a third major political party and we need common sense economic policies. We must, we must, we must create a free labor market. We don't need third class population which cannot afford to buy goods and services for the only reason there is no free labor market. We need to simplify the tax code at least ten times. One thousand pages of tax codes must be limited. We as a nation, we spend too much money on services which are not necessary. We cannot consume accountants, and we cannot export them.

We should determine once and forever what government services we need and how much. Looting of tax dollars must stop. If we decide we want government to deliver something, we have to pay upon delivery. There is no communism. Not yet. We have to give third class population third class medical care, and sure it will cost something. I'd bet a dollar if we could stop looting of tax dollars, there would be enough money for this program.

We need election law reform. PIGs should not be allowed to buy politicians. One dollar-per-voter limit must be imposed as soon as possible. Third party exists. Working poor and unemployed, welfare recipients, we all belong to this party. There are many millions of us, who are part of the third world population living in this first class country. We need a third party approach to the problems of this country which are mostly our problems. We should take the best of both parties. We should believe in a free market, as Republicans do. We should believe in social security, as Democrats do.

We should not believe in PIGs. Money politics should be abandoned. Money should be collected for any purpose. All of us should work for the election campaigns of third party candidates as volunteers. It's time to have at least one party which is not for sale. Democrats who believe in a free labor market! Organize political clubs of third party in every apartment building and every work place. As soon as money is involved, the party will serve only those few who have access to that money. The third party should have an army of volunteers.

How much time it will take for the part to become a real force? As much time as we need to educate a large part of the population. As soon as it is done, the third party will become a third major political party in this country.

CHAPTER

21 DEMOCRATS VERSUS REPUBLICANS

The question is not which political party is better. Democrats are the tax-and-loot people. Republicans are the don't tax-but-loot party. The question is which political party is worse. You may know all there is in economics, and you may still not be able to answer the question.

The author of this book did not vote in the November 8, 1994 elections. Liberal politician Nita Lowey was running against conservative business lawyer Andy Hartzell. What is worse, a liberal politician or a business lawyer? This is not immediately obvious.

Politicians of both parties are bought by special interest groups which pay for their re-election campaigns. We should call them political interest groups or PIGs for short. They still get something in return and that something maybe many times bigger than what was paid as a contribution to the election campaign. Looking for a great return on your money being invested? Invest in an election campaign!

We need campaign finance reform in this country. Our present politicians in public office work for political interest groups. These so-called PIGS contributed money to political campaigns and they hired lobbyists to peddle their influences. At election time, the politicians want your vote and they make campaign promises.

When the election is over, it is back to business as usual.

CHAPTER

22   ITALIAN ECONOMICS

In Italy, there is a shortage of politicians. Chickens cost too much money and the Italians demand higher wages. Government prints more money and gives it to them. When more money is pumped into the economy, the price of chickens will go up. Inflation is not good and inflation means that you need more money to buy the same amount of chickens.

When the workers go out on strike, they would demand more money in the form of wages. The government refuses to give in to their demands and they will vote it down. Almost every week there is a new administration in power which can print more money than that past administration. The average Italian is a millionaire and the minimum wage in Italy is at one million liras a month. A chicken cost one thousand liras.

The Italians hoped to find government which will give them as much money as they want. What about inflation? Italians said, "No problem." If there is inflation, this means government is no good. In a free country like Italy, we can always vote it down. This is the Italian mentality.

CHAPTER

23 UNEMPLOYMENT

Why is there so much unemployment? Not everybody has a house. Not everybody has a car and not everybody has even a room to live in. Let us hire some people to build those houses and cars. Not so simple and there is a picture of reality. For example, there are thousands of people in Harlem on welfare who really want to work. Why not build a General Motors manufacturing plant in Harlem and put more people to work? They would work for ten dollars per hour. GM would save a lot of money on labor costs. Savings would be passed on the consumer and we would have just what we dream about--affordable new cars and community resident working in a manufacturing plant. It used to be like that. What was good for GM was always good for America.

General Motors will not build a manufacturing plant in Harlem. If supply of cars is increased too much, the price of those cars will do down. When prices go down, there will be no maximum profit. Every industry is interested in maximizing profits. They don't want to hire unemployed people. This is the real reason why there is unemployment.

CHAPTER

24 BUSINESS CYCLE

Every 7 to 10 years there is an economic recession. An economic recession means that the production of goods and services declines. Businesses "downsize" people out of the door, and unemployed people spend very little money on goods and services. Many who are still employed, fear that they may soon lose their jobs and they also spend less money. When everybody spends less money, there is less demand for goods and services so that the recession feeds upon itself. If this process continues long enough, then any country will find itself in a depression. A depression is a severe recession.

What are the causes of the recession? We will take a good look at different views. Some people would say, "Immigrants take jobs away from Americans." Is it really true? Suppose the island of Great Britain began to go under and the Brits arrived in the USA, so that the population of the United States increased twicefold. Will they be unemployed? No. We need twice as many houses, twice as many cars, twice as much food and clothing. We will need twice as much government. There will be twice as many jobs and maybe, even more than double. Historically, as the population of the United States doubles, the size of the government increases five times. This would be a good chance to "reinvent government"[1] and that why total number of jobs created would be more than the total number of jobs in Great Britain before they moved to the United States.

---

[1] In 1992/1993 there has been a discussion about how to reinvent government.

Seriously, nobody knows it for sure.

What is known for sure is that the number of jobs is directly proportionate to the size of the population. In China, there are so many more jobs, because there are so many more people to house, feed and clothed. As simple as it is, that is should we tell the Brits that if something goes wrong with their island, they would be better off learning Spanish. English is good enough as a second language to learn.

What are the consequences of immigration? It is not the loss of jobs, and it is not a recession. The conflict is not economic but it is mostly cultural. The conflict is very real, and "English as a second language" is an example of pure stupidity. Every American should know some Spanish as a second language, and not the other way around. Anyway, this cultural conflict should not be dramatized. We should remember that gradually the American continent will become a common market. Good Spanish will be a very big plus to do business with Spanish speaking countries.

What about illegal immigration? The State of California spends a lot of money on public education and medical care. To answer this question, let us go back to the basics of economics.

Every economic system has to produce goods and services so that they can be distributed to the population. Free market economy is like a big table. Everybody bring something to the table whatever goods or services he is producing and takes from the table whatever the free market is willing to give him for his goods or services. The medium of exchange is money. The more contribution you make to the system, and the more you should get back from the system.

The system is not perfect and it is not even good enough. Some people are taking from the system many times more than they put back into the system. For example, custodians in the New York City public schools are doing a job which many people with a college education would be happy to do for half the wages that custodians are getting at this present time. They cannot go there and say, "Hey, I will do the same job for half the wages, and I'll do it better. Fire this man and hire me!"

Why can't they do this? There is a labor union whose members are paid whatever they demand, in terms of wages. Not whatever a free market is willing to pay. Let us compare what a unionized custodian and an illegal immigrant would bring to the free market table, and what they take back from that table.

Illegal immigrants work for two or three dollars an hour on a plantation. We should take in account that for the economy there is no difference. What is the immigration status of this low-life, picking vegetables on a plantation? As long as he contributes something to the economy, he is a positive factor. He brings vegetables to the free market table and he is entitled to get his two or three dollars an hour. What is wrong with illegal immigrants? Are some of them criminals? Are there more criminals than among U.S. citizens? If there are twice more criminals among illegal immigrants, this problem should be addressed. Either seal the border or build a few labor camps, where criminals would do productive work and pay for staying in the prison labor camp.

Some people say the State of California paid so much money for public education and public health. The taxpayers paid medical benefits for the illegal immigrants and it will be better to cut them off. They should not be allowed to bring vegetables to the table, and to take two or three dollars from the table. They shouldn't have free access to public school education or municipal hospitals. Is this fair? At a first glance, it is perfectly fair. Illegal immigrants don't pay taxes, and schools and public hospitals are supported by taxes collected from legal residents. Illegal immigrants get a free ride.

But we should notice that there is a problem. Suppose they were perfectly legal residents. In this case, they would be entitled to minimum wage and public school education and Medicaid programs. In other words, they would make the same contribution to the table of the free market economy but would take back two or three times more. Once again, the immigration status doesn't matter as far as economy is concerned.

This brings us to the next question. Maybe low wage workers should not be entitled to minimum wages, public education and municipal hospitals? Get your two dollars an hour, no schools and nothing? It becomes very complicated.

What in the hell is he bringing to the table of the free market economy? We have thousands of people who would do it for half of those wages. Just give them a chance to work! We should know that a unionized labor force is not just labor. It is the finest labor. They are entitled to higher wages than low-lifes. How much higher? Nobody knows for sure. We should tell them, "Folks," your time is up! Illegal immigrants are chased out and there is going to be a lot of openings on California plantations. You will be entitled to work for minimum wages, public housing, public education and public hospitals."

We don't need redistribution of wealth after it has been distributed but we need justice at the moment the wealth is distributed.

We read every day about the hungry, the poor, the less fortunate, disadvantaged and so on and on. Their disadvantage is to live in a society where there is no free labor market. They are not fortunate enough to have free access to the labor market. This is the reason why they are poor and hungry. Let us chase the public school custodians all the way to the California plantations and give their $70,000 a year jobs to the people who will be happy to do this job for only $35,000 a year. Those people will be happy to do this job for only $35,000 a year. Those people don't need public assistance and soup kitchens. All they need is free access to the labor market. All they need is an opportunity to contribute something to the table and take something back from the table, whatever the free market is willing to pay them.

We need a law which would allow any qualified unemployed person to take the job that he wants and be able to do well, for half wages.

The American economy now consist of roughly five economies. At the bottom, there are people making around $5 per hour and they are really third class citizens. They live in third class neighborhoods. They consume third class goods and services, and live in a third class society.

There is a part of the economy which is oriented to produce goods and services for this segment of the population. The South Bronx is an example of such a neighborhood, which consists of $5 per hour people, mostly without health care. They are making $10,000 a year in income and cannot afford to buy any medical insurance. When they get sick, they go to the municipal hospitals and pay nothing because they have nothing to pay with. Preventive medical care would be much cheaper, but this society doesn't know how to put their tax dollars to better use.

Now we should ask ourselves, "Do these people contribute less to the society than $70,000 a year custodians?" No. These people don't have free access to the labor market and that is the reason why they are on the bottom.

On the next level, there are second class citizens. They make around $10 per hour or $20,000 a year in income. They are much better than a third class citizen. If they can afford to buy a new car once in a lifetime, any illness in a family will put them in bankruptcy. Medical insurance is good for healthy people. As soon as you become sick, you will have to sell that used car to the third class citizen to pay for your medical bills.

On the next level, there are first class citizens. They make around $20 per hour or $40,000 a year in income. There people can afford to buy a house, a good car and good medical insurance.

Somewhat at $100,000 a year, people are rich, and those making a million dollars a year are super rich. There are extremely poor people in this society. And there are extremely rich. Can we help the poor by confiscating some wealth? We can tell Bill Gates, "Hey, you've got nine billion dollars and there are so many people to feed. We are going to take away your nine billion dollars to feed the hungry." Would it help to feed the hungry? Yes, it would seem so.

Suppose Bill Gates makes one billion dollar a year. He can consume one billion chickens at wholesale prices or 1 million cows, or whatever. It's not fair! And he is not supposed to eat so much! Let's take those cows out of his mouth and give them to the hungry!

The only problem is that he doesn't have a million cows. He cannot eat hundreds of cows at lunch. He has so much paper money that he doesn't take from the table even a small portion of what he could afford to eat. He takes from the table, not millions of cows, but mostly paper money. What can we take out of his mouth? Just a big bag of paper money.

The hungry don't eat paper. They want bread and butter, meat and potatoes. Sure, we can take all the paper money from all the billionaires but it will be just an Italian game. More paper money chasing the same number of chickens. You will simply need more money chasing the same number of chickens. You will simply need more money to buy the same chicken.

The more money billionaires have, the less that paper money has any difference for the economy. If billionaires had their wealth in a form of cows and chicken, there would be no problem to feed the hungry. Just impose a goods confiscating tax on those billions of chickens and you've got the problem solved.

Big bad Bill chasing and consuming flying cows... It would make a good screen saver or a computer game. But it has no connection with virtual reality. And now we are still at the same closed door. Why are so many people poor and hungry? Why are millions of Americans, eager to go to work, still unemployed?

We all know that the more goods and services we produce, the more we will consume. You have to produce something only if there is demand for it. Demand for housing is not our desire to live in better housing. Demand means amount of money out there chasing housing. If there is no money, you will not be able to sell them at a profit. Unemployed people don't have money to buy houses. No money means no demand. No demand means that nobody will hire the unemployed to build the houses. It means that the unemployed will stay unemployed. Should it be this way? Where is the beginning of the chain?

The beginning of the chain is at the closed door. The closed door is the door, which lead to the free labor market. The closed door means that you cannot enter the labor market. You cannot earn your living and you will always be treated as a third class citizen.

A third class citizen cannot buy a new car, which is manufactured by first-class citizens. Everybody know that third world countries cannot afford to buy goods manufactured in first world countries.

Basically the same story is true in the United States. Closed door means closed opportunities. The problem with this is that third class citizens cannot afford to buy anything, which is bad for the economy. If there was a free labor market, everybody would get as much money as he deserve, not as much as he demands. Cars and houses would cost some 30-40% less. But this is not so much important. What is more important? The big gap in income between first-class and third class citizens would be reduced. Poor people would be able to obtain mortgages to buy homes. A house manufactured by $20 per hour labor force costs much more than a house manufactured by $10 per hour labor force. Cheaper housing would be more affordable to the people. We don't have to cry about Bill Gate's big house. We have to give those third class citizens cheaper homes. We have to build them, literally. If we don't create a free market for labor, "less fortunate" people will become even more "less fortunate."

We have millions of people on welfare. If we count them as unemployed they really are, then the unemployment rate will be close to 10 percent. It means that 1 out of every 10 people is not working. This is a real waste of economic resources. If 10 million unemployed and welfare recipients laid one brick each day (a day!), it would build a house bigger than Bill Gate's house. Why not put the people to work building houses for them-selves?

We should note that unemployment is not just unemployment. It causes the whole specter of problems that we are so fed up with. Drugs, crime and broken families are just a few of them. Unemployed people eventually go on welfare. They would be happy to bring something to the table but they are not allowed to work. It is clear to everybody that the more houses we build, the cheaper they will be, the better for us? Yes, it is clear to everybody.

What is exactly the problem? Construction labor unions don't want to increase supply of housing. If supply of new housing increases, the price of homes still decrease. If the price of new houses decreases, the price of labor used in construction will decrease accordingly. Who wants to reduce his own wages? Nobody.

The United Auto Workers Union doesn't want to increase supply of new cars. Cheaper houses and cars are good for us but not so good for them. It's us against them in this not so free economy.

And now let us find the differences between ideally organized economy and economy of the United States. In an ideally organized economy, everybody works and brings to the table whatever he is capable of bringing. The more we bring to the table, the more we take from the table. Un-employment rates should not be higher than one or two percent because the more people work and bring something to the table, the richer we will all be. The real wealth is not paper money. The real wealth are those houses, cars, good highways and most of all, a smart educated population. If the population of the United States were educated enough, there would be less of a problem in putting people to work.

The difference between ideally organized economy and economy of the United States is that able bodies are allowed to be idle. Poor people can't have anything, and they are entitled only to soup kitchens. Do we need more soup kitchens to help the poor and hungry? No. We don't need charities.

In an ideally organized economy, workers are able to buy each other's products because they are paid according to their contribution to the economy, not according to their demands.

In the United States, we have an economy where third and second-class citizens cannot afford to buy those products which are produced by first-class workers. The third and second-class workers don't have access to the labor market of the first-class. It creates inequality in wages. What, if anything, may be done to better organize the United States economy?

Probably, nobody will be able to organize it better than a strict free market, where a gap in wages is reduced to a level at which third class labor is able to consume more products, which are not affordable to them now. A big gap in wages will exist as long as there is no free market for labor. As we see, free market for labor is more important for the poor than all charities and soup kitchens combined.

In a sense, free market policies of Ronald Reagan were more important to the poor than to the rich. There were big achievements, and there were big mistakes. We will return to that thought later.

As for now, we are still discussing a business cycle. Why there is no stability? There is a boom and there is eventually a bust. We know by now that the instability of the system has nothing to do with immigrants stealing jobs from Americans. It has nothing to do with millions of welfare recipients who are not given access to a free labor market.

To understand the nature of instability, we should understand the role money has played in the economy. The role of money in the economy is that of blood in the living organism. Blood brings oxygen and nutrition to parts of the body.

When an economy is in good shape, people spend more money. They spend what they had saved during a recession. The second half of 1994 is a good example. They spend more money than they earn. When everybody spends more than they earn, prices will go up. Houses, cars, and eventually everything will become more expensive. Now everybody knows that a year from now everything will even be more expensive. So it's better to buy it now. When prices go up, it will last two or three years, until savings are well spent. Everybody who had money, already bought whatever he wanted. This moment is very interesting. The economy seems to be in excellent shape. Whatever political party occupies the White House, everybody will be listening to how knowledgeable they are about the economy and bla-bla-bla. A knowledgeable observer will notice that the money which was accumulated by the population during bad times is already spent. Prices are going higher and there is much less money chasing the goods.

The economy is not in a recession yet, technically. The population doesn't understand what is happening. Many people are still taking mortgages to buy houses at a peak of the price. They believe that prices will go up and up forever. As money runs out, the economy runs out of steam. Politicians blame each other. People hear about economic problems and spend even less money. Everybody wants to save some money. Nobody buys houses and cars. And the rest is familiar enough. People are losing jobs and they cannot afford to pay mortgages anymore. Their homes and cars are sold at auction prices. Every 1 out of 10 people are unemployed. Those nine who are still working, save money and everybody tries to figure out who is to blame. Immigrants! Welfare recipients! Nobody wants to think that it might be their own stupidity, which is to blame for buying houses at the peak of the price and then losing their jobs. Smart people buy houses during the recession. Stupid people buy houses when the economy is okay. 1995 and beyond is a good time for stupid people to buy houses. Smart people will save money during good times to buy a house at bad times. If most people were smart, there would be no recessions.

It is very important to understand that elementary economics knowledge is absolutely necessary for every American. It should be taught in every junior high school in this country. We are all in one boat and we should not let this boat take on water on either side. If we go under, we will go under together. There is no safer side in this boat.

As we see, the major cause of the recession is our low education in our high schools and probably, in most colleges. Most people act like they don't know that the same house will be sold much cheaper and interest rates will be lower. It would be much more fun to buy this house during a recession.

What is the role of labor unions? When economy becomes better after the recession, prices go up from the depressed levels of recession. When the prices go up, it is inflation. It is the same Italian game: "Give me more money because I can't buy a chicken." When price of chicken goes up again, there is no problem for them. Just give them more money. We suffer from the inflation? The unionized worker doesn't suffer. They will always get more money to buy the same chicken. It's the third class population, who suffers the most, and the labor aristocracy.

We should understand that inflation stimulates the economy. As prices go higher, people decide to buy before it's too late. The more people buy houses the more the prices of the houses go up. When unions demand more money and get more money in a form of higher wages, the higher wages contribute to the inflation rate. The higher the inflation rate, the more people will decide to buy. There is one problem with money, the tact is that money and luck always run out. As soon as money runs out, the economy runs out of luck. It's not so much important how many house have been built or are going to be built--that's bull. It's how much money is still out there chasing houses. The role of labor unions is to go on strike when inflations picks up. The strikes contribute to the inflation rate when there is not so much money out of the economy and then, we are done.

We should understand that spending money in the economy should be like running a marathon. If you run too fast, you will eventually run out of breath.

There is not enough oxygen and fuel in the blood. Oxygen debt is building up and you have to slow down. You cannot spend more oxygen than the amount delivered by the blood, for a long period of time. Oxygen debt must be repaid. You've got to catch your breath. Our economy is very much like a stupid marathon runner who is running in an on-again, off-again style. According to statistics, running a marathon maybe fatal for the system. The on-again, off-again style in our economic marathon is called a business cycle.

CHAPTER

25 ABOUT HEALTH CARE

They say that health care is not affordable for everybody in this country. Let us take a good look at this problem. We all know that all goods and services cost something. We also know that every person in our class society consumes goods and services according to their income. People with higher income consumer better goods and services and there is nothing wrong with it. As long as money is made fairly.

The fact is that the third class population consumes third class goods and services. The second class population consumes second class goods and services and so on. Now let's take a look at who doesn't have health care and why. We should notice that health care may be classified like all goods and services. There are first class things and there are third class things. It would be wrong to say that the third class population should get first class medical care. We are talking about third class medical care for the third class population doesn't have health care. If this country were populated by better educated people, this problem would had been solved a long time ago. There is a lot of discussion in this country about the way health care should be provided. Some say that government is not efficient enough to run our health care system. The Soviet government had collapsed because there was no free market. Government-owned enterprises cannot be run efficiently.

This logic is defective and government-owned enterprises may be very effective. The Soviet space program is one example, which private firm built those submarines with nuclear missiles. Both government and private enterprises may be very effective. The U.S. Army is another example and nobody stood against government more firmly than Ronald Reagan. He had his surgery in the military hospital which is a perfect example of government medical care. There is government and there is no government. We should distinguish between them.

Efficiency of capitalist and socialist systems are going to be the subjects of another book. For the purpose of this book would be enough to say that capitalism in Brazil is not going to be nearly as effective as socialism in Russia. You may ease or tighten monetary policy in Brazil. You may increase or decrease interest rates. You may inject as much money as you wish in the economy and at the end, you are not going to have much of a difference. The problem is that you cannot take from the table more than what you put on it. Some financial institutions may put a dollar on the table and take back five dollars but a nation as a whole, cannot do it. The standard of living of any nation depends on the productivity of work. The more goods are produced, and the more goods are brought to the table. The rest is distribution and redistribution of income. This is called "money games." The Soviet Union was actually alone against so many great nations for a long time. How come? This question is not answered yet. The Soviet Union had bad government and the system was immoral. Confrontation against the whole world was stupid. We are not talking about morality of the system but we are talking about efficiency of government.

This is not a very simple problem which has no simple answer.

There are many variables involved there. One problem is that most of the creative and smart people work for the private sector. People like Michael Milkin make millions of dollars on Wall Street and the rest work for government. How can we expect smart people to work for the government?

The biggest problem is financing health care reform. Who will pay for it? Let us take a look at who pays for health care now. The United Auto Workers Union members have good benefits including health insurance. Who pays for health insurance? No, not Ford. Not General Motors. The costs are passed on to the consumer and at the end, we will pay for it. Health care costs are included in the price of every car. People in the third class need lifetime savings to buy a new car. They don't have any type of healthcare. The third class population pays for first class healthcare of the labor aristocrats. When an aristocrat goes to a fast food restaurant, he doesn't want to pay a quarter more for the price of hamburger to cover healthcare cost of the third class population. It doesn't make sense. We should pay for each other's health insurance. You buy health insurance for your employees, your competitor across the street doesn't buy health care, then he has an advantage over you. You may be out of business before long. This is the reason why we need mandated health care. In this case, both you and your competitor across the street would be mandated by law to buy insurance for your employees. The insurance policy will not be as good as the United Auto Workers. We are talking about third class medical care. Who will pay for it? If everybody is mandated, everybody will pass those additional costs on to the consumer. Will we stop buying hamburgers at a higher price? Yes. Exactly as we should stop buying those overpriced cars.

The best way would be to extend the Medicaid program to the working poor. It is very simple math. There is not enough money to give a big cut to the insurance industry. Taxes? We already know that taxes are not bad but the looting of tax dollars is bad. For the insurance industry, all of the money which doesn't trickle down is bad. We should remind them that Ronald Reagan knew better. He trusted himself to government enterprise. Why shouldn't we? We should understand that the medical insurance industry and the medical care industry are two different industries. As a result, there will always be insurance fraud. The medical industry is not interested in cutting costs as long as insurance companies pay for everything. If an insurance company buys a hospital and sells medical insurance to the public, then in this case insurance companies have real control over unnecessary costs. Even this would not solve the problem. There are too many malpractice lawyers chasing too few doctors. The result is a good chain, where big animals prey upon smaller animals. In a medical food chain, lawyers consume insurance companies, insurance companies consume doctors and doctors consume patients. It's a jungle out there and doctors are not the biggest animals. Some big animals must be cut out of the food supply entirely.

Another problem is that people don't want to pay for medical insurance until they get old and sick. People from the ages of 20-60 say, "Why should we pay more taxes for other people's medical care." After the age of 60, when people are sick enough to see a doctor every other day, and they say, "Why is medical insurance so expensive?"

There is a big difference between auto insurance and medical insurance. Every owner of an automobile is required to have insurance by state law. When some of the motorists are involved in automobile accidents, and they are covered. They may get more money than they have contributed to the insurance pool because other people have also contributed to the pool. With medical insurance, there is a different story. Nobody wants to pay until there is a medical emergency. Which, they want to buy enough medical coverage equivalent to a Lexus. The same amount of money which could buy only used Honda Civic. Get real, folks would you? There is no such thing as a free lunch. Everybody has to pay either more taxes to cover medical costs of government or buy private insurance. Don't wait until you are 60 years old to buy medical coverage. This way, everybody would contribute to the insurance pool and everybody would be covered in case of a medical emergency. There is no big difference between private medical insurance and government run Medicare and Medicare programs. Both private and government programs take money in and give out medical services. The problem is to determine who can give more medical care for a buck. This buck must be paid that there should be no question about it.

Government in the United States is discredited and too many crooks out there are looting tax dollars. It doesn't mean that government is always bad.

Some doctors are looting both government funded Medicaid and private insurance. We should not have stereotypes. We should look at who is looting and how much. Looting is caused by many people, and businesses lose a lot of money. This is the reason why government hospitals are overcharging the patient. It is a good enough solution to deliver third class medical care to the third class population of this country.

In order to make Medicaid affordable, a monthly premium of $40 per month will be charged to each individual. Services from Medicaid will include long-term care, dental care, eyeglasses, prescription drugs, home care and emergency room service.

This illustration will explain who New York State can save money on Medicaid.

Premium = $40 per month per individual	$40
New Yorkers who paid monthly premiums	X 6,000,00
Total monthly premium income	240,000,00
	X12
Yearly premium income	2,880,000,000

The total comes out to $2.8 billion

This is an example of how New York State will save money in Medicaid costs when fraud and waste are eliminated from this program. This illustration showed us that state and local government doesn't have to contribute a cent into the Medicaid program without the bureaucratic mess.

CHAPTER

26 WHY I DID NOT VOTE

Before the November 8, 1994 elections, the coauthor of this book received three brochures from Andy Hartzell, a Republican candidate for Congress from the 18th Congressional District in New York.

Those brochures informed me about his political agenda and about Nita Lowey's liberal agenda. Let us take a good look at these brochures which I am going to keep as an example of cheap propaganda.

"My generation has lived the American dream. I want to make sure the next generation can too." Good intention! This is Andy Hartzells' 10-point plan to restore growth and bring new jobs to Westchester County, Bronx and Queens.

Point One: "Oppose increases in federal income taxes." It sounds good but the federal government needs money in order to operate. Too much money is being looted everyday and this is a big problem. There is nothing in the plan to oppose the looting of income taxes. We don't need lower taxes and we don't need higher taxes. We need to collect as much tax as we need. The problem is that money should be spent well for the benefit of the whole country. As simple as it may be.

Point Two: "Oppose unfunded federal and state mandates which cause skyrocketing local property taxes." There are too many mandates which are funded and unfunded. The whole system is messed up and it should be simplified. The problem is in Congress itself. Any mandate, funded or unfunded costs money. A funded mandated means that a state receive a lot of money from the federal government. An unfunded mandate means that money should be collected locally. The money will be spent locally, too. Who will receive it? Those business firms which contributed to the campaign of the congressman. We are talking about money here. As long as business firms are allowed to buy Congressmen, there will be more and more mandates, both funded and unfunded. This is are real problem with mandates.

Point Three: "Allow $500 per child in come tax credit which would save the average working family in the 18th Congressional District over $1,000 a year." This proposal is equivalent to reducing taxes for everybody. Do we need lower taxes? Yes. Let us take one more look at what taxes are used for. This money is used for our national defense, which is vital for this country. Police and fire-fighters are paid by tax dollars. Social Services waste a lot of money. Social Security, Medicaid and Medicare are the biggest programs. There is a huge debt that the federal government pays interest on. Should we cut social programs? Yes, we should but not before there is a free market for labor and everybody has access to it. Yes, welfare is very bad and we should abolish it altogether. The next generation should know about welfare only from the history books. The problem is that we cannot abolish their evil welfare programs until there are jobs for welfare recipients. Jobs will be there on the same day when we have a free market for labor. We should understand that in economics everything is connected. We cannot cut taxes because we need money for social service programs. We cannot cut social services because people cannot find jobs. People cannot find jobs because there is no free market. There are many educated people who cannot find a job. Simply, there are not enough jobs in the economy. It sounds like nonsense. We need houses, cars, and all kinds of durable goods because there is no demand for those goods. There is no demand because the unemployed Americans don't have money to buy. They don't have money because they didn't find any work. The problem evolve in a circle. The very first step to break this circle is to create free labor market. We need to cut taxes and to give tax credits. We must not give politicians bribes in order to get elected to public office. We have to put all of the people to work. There is only one way to do it. We must create a free market for labor and everything else is nonsense.

Point Four: "Create enterprise zones in areas that have suffered dramatic job loss." Everybody wants to pay less taxes and enterprise zones will steal jobs from other locations and they don't create new jobs. If we give the South Bronx a status of an "enterprise zone" with low or no taxes, some businesses will relocate there from other parts of the city. It doesn't mean that local residents will be employed there. Even so, new jobs are created and old jobs are simply relocated. The concern of unemployment is spread more evenly. The only gain is tax savings for those businesses which have contributed to the election campaign of Mr. Hartzell. The problem is that we have to collect a certain amount of money. If some business get tax credits in those silly enterprise zones, it means that others have to contribute more. The end result is that taxes are reduced for those who have contributed to the campaign of Mr. Hartzell, while taxes are increased for those who did not contributed. Mr. Hartzell is a business lawyer. He is really concerned that his clients pay high taxes. He is also an author of the book, "Treacherous Snows." Why not write another book like, "Treacherous Economics?"

Point Five: "Encourage businesses to buy new equipment, machinery and modernize facilities by indexing depreciation schedules." As if there are not enough accounting tricks, Mr. Hartzell wants more of them. We have more than ten thousand pages of tax codes. There are more than enough accounting tricks and loopholes about not paying taxes. Do we need any more? No, we do not. It is just the opposite and we need to get rid of them. They all sound as good as enterprise zones but the truth is, that the only gain is for those few who contribute. Society as a whole is losing. When a business firm hires an accounting firm, a few business lawyers try to write all the wrong things in a tax code. As we know from treacherous economics, all of the costs are passed on to the consumer. Who is the consumer? It's me. I don't want to pay even one cent to every Hartzell out there. Nobody asks me whether or not I want them. The costs for those accountants and tax lawyers are included in the price of everything that I consume as a consumer. This is one of the reason why the average Joe is consumed.

Point Six: "Make permanent the Research and Development Tax Credit." This is a very good idea. We have to make sure that this credit goes to high technology firms, not to advertising, accounting and law firms.

Point Seven: "Ease restrictions on banks to encourage new business lending." This was done exactly a decade ago. Restrictions were eased so much that every crook and criminal was able to get a big loan. The result is that nobody now knows how much money has been looted and transferred to Swiss bank accounts. Some people believe that they have a constitutional right to borrow money from a bank for whatever purpose. Nobody knows how many fraudulent corporations have been created in the 1980's with the sole purpose to loot money. Those fraudulent corporations went bankrupt and the crooks who created them walked away with the loot. Lending money to new businesses was a code word for looting. The problem is that the federal government has certain obligations regarding the banking system. Banks are in business to borrow money from one party and to lend it to another party. These activities are determined by the supply and demand for money. What a sweet world it would be if everybody demand for money were satisfied. It doesn't work that way. When a bank makes too many bad loans, it may find itself in bankruptcy. Deposits are insured by the federal government and the federal government is supported by taxpayers. Why should I pay more taxes for your clients' bad business judgement or outright looting? I don't need any redistribution of my income. Business lending is not prohibited. If you have a business, people stand in line to get your goods or services, believe me that all the banks will stand in line to lend money to you. If you want to saturate an already saturated market, your demand for money is not good. Restrictions mean just that--restrictions on bad demand. They may seem to be cruel and unusual punishment, but so is the experience when Savings and Loan collapsed. Do we need anymore looting?

Point Eight: "Reduce Capital Gains Tax to provide fresh investment capital to create jobs and reduce unemployment." Once again, we have to collect a certain amount of money. As simple as it is. We know that to much of taxpayer's money is looted. The collapse of the Savings and Loan banks is a good example. Crooks walked away with bags of money, and taxpayers are left holding the bag. What does this business lawyer want in point Seven of this plan? "Ease restrictions on banks to encourage new business lending." It means that banks should more easily lend some people other people's money. Other people's money is not at risk. It is insured by the government. Government can guaranteed this money only because it will be collected from the average Joe or John. What is really at risk? It's average Joe's money. What do we see in Point Eight? It's average Joe's money. What do we see in Point Eight? Reduce Capital Gains Tax on capital which was guaranteed by average Joe. If the business went belly up, Joe pays. If money is made, taxes should be low. Point Eight is an example of pure propaganda. There is no evidence whatsoever that lower taxes will created jobs and reduce unemployment.

Point Nine: "Require the federal government to perform cost-benefit analysis on new regulations before they are implemented." Sure, there are too many regulations. There are too may lawyers in Congress who create too many regulations. There are too few economists in Congress who could "perform cost-benefit analysis." All the analysis are performed by economists for special interest groups, and the role of Congressman is to lobby for them. One more lawyer in Congress is like on more lobbyists.

Point Ten: "Repeal Social Security earnings limitation which forces working seniors aged 65-69 to pay higher taxes." The Social Security program has been created to give an average Joe some social security. There are some people who make the same amount of money after they work. They will make the same amount of money after they retire. Do they need any social security? No. They already have it. This is not to say that they don't deserve what they make. Some of them certainly do, and there are many who don't. Tax lawyers and accountants will help you pay less or no taxes. They make money before and after retirement. What do they contribute to the table? We can ask ourselves if Bill Gates deserves his billions. He sells his software all over the world and pumps money into the Unites States. He delivers a product we need. The product may be consumed, exported and the product is tangible. We cannot consume lawyers and we cannot export lawyers. This 10-point plan would not help most of us to live the American dream. This is plan not to pay taxes. Nine points of this plan call for tax cut, and this position is respectable. The only point missed is spending cuts. Tax cuts without spending cuts will result in increased budget deficits. A budget deficit means that government must borrow money. Borrowed money must be returned with interest. Who will pay for it? The next generation, according to this business lawyer. We must pay our debt. Paying off that debt should not be the American dream for the next generation.

CHAPTER

27 HOW TO COMMUNICATE

We are approaching the 21st century. Science and technology are means of communications more affordable for the average American. We can communicate now by fax machines, computer and voice mail. What should be our message?

America is a bad country with unemployment and crime... We hit new lows and we should take a look around. Our new laws are still higher than other countries' new highs. America is still the best country in the world and people risk their lives to become Americans. To them, America is not an object in space and time. America is a symbol of freedom.

Pioneers of this country, as soon as they smelled other people's fire. They knew it was time to move to the new frontier. Americans are these kind of people. Today, as hundred of years went by, we look for new frontiers. There are a lot of barriers and people are not educated enough to understand politicians. Too often people are taken for a ride. We have hundreds of thousand of college kids who are educated enough not be taken for a ride. As soon as we begin discussions in colleges and universities, the new journey has just begun. The truth will not be out. Nobody can claim monopoly on the truth. Nobody knows exactly which way we should go. We must move one step at a time. One way or another, we will get there to higher ground.

Many countries have economic problems. Unemployment in Europe is much higher than in the United States. Why not them? The answer is simple enough. Europe cannot do it alone. Europe is a symbol and it is a symbol of the status-quo. There are talking about free market labor but the problem is a free market without a free labor market is nonsense. Labor unions will simply demonstrate all over Europe demanding more money. As soon as inflation hits, they may strap the European government and they will begin a shootout. There is going to be a big mess out there.

Europeans cannot establish a free labor market. For them, they would like for their grandfathers to leave everything in Europe hundreds of years ago and move to the Wild West. The Wild West is not part of Europe culture. It was not a purpose of this book to explain everything about economics. Rather, the purpose is to encourage individuals who are able to think and to take charge in leadership of themselves and masses of people.

At this time, economics is a liberal art course, and not a science course. We simply don't know enough of how the economic functions. We cannot form any meaningful economic policy unless we understand economics. The science of economic is still like the Wild West and we have to explore it.

There are more simple questions than answers and not every simple question has a simple answer. What is the effect of taxes on the economy? What is the effect of not having a free labor market? How deliberating for the economy is our habit to spend at good times and not to spend money at bad times? Why not spend money at bad times, when everything is cheaper? A part of the answer is that if everybody spends money at the bad times, then bad times will become good times, and good times will become bad times. The real question is how to spend money at a constant rate, so that accelerated spending doesn't create a situation when prices are high because of recent accelerated spending. There is not much money to spend because of the same reason.

Don't we need a better monetary policy? Should we blame there President for the economy? The Federal Reserve Bank, our central bank is semi-independent of the President.

If George Bush was more informed about the economy, he would insist on lowering interest rates at the very beginning of his term. What is the reason? Economy is not good enough. Interest rates are too high and people cannot afford to take mortgages at good rates. We need lower rates in order to give a boost to the economy.

As soon as people hear something like this, they stop spending. Some of them are concerned about their jobs, and they want to save money for the bad times. Some of them want to wait until interest rates are at their lowest. They don't buy big ticket items until they are told that the interest rate party is over. For the next couple of years, there will be a recession. A lot of money will be accumulated. At that point, start raising interest rates and everybody was waiting with bags of money is suddenly on the market. Everybody is buying everything!

Economic miracle! Bush would be elected for a second term. Instead, interest rates went down too late for George Bush to get re-elected. He was taken for a ride probably. Now we have interest rates rising and the economy is booming. What is next? It's not economy stupid! It's our stupidity!

We have the best information system in the world. College kids will now have access to unlimited amounts of statistics. And they have what it takes to go where not many people have been. This book is not the answer to all of economic and political questions of the world, but they must be answered. We must answer because we are Americans. We are the New World.

A part of the answer should be a third party. We already know enough to make our economy better. We should educate as many people as possible.

Probably, many people will still ask questions, which are not answered in this book. Those questions will be answered in the second edition of this book which will be better organized by topics. All economic problems which are simple enough to understand for the average American, *WILL BE ANSWERED.

CHAPTER

28

THE SOLUTIONS

What happens when you employed welfare recipients to build houses? Those welfare recipients will acquire a new skill in the construction trade. As a result, a drop in the unemployment rate will be effected by the increase in employment. The same result can also happen in other industries. The number of people on welfare rolls will decrease. The welfare recipients need a hand up, not a hand out. This is actually a good example of welfare reform.

What happens when the supply of real estate is increased? Houses will be more available for home buyers. The price of a house will drop dramatically and prices of existing homes will also drop to keep up with the competition. As a result, the Federal Reserve Board will have to lower the prime lending rate that they charged banks to borrow money. The money will flow freely through the economy.

The basic construction materials for building new houses will be cheaper.

How will construction companies benefit from this? Wages of construction workers will be lower due to the increase supply of the labor pool. The construction companies will also have to place lower bids for construction contracts so that competition will also increased.

How will this benefit real estate developers? Government on the federal, state and local level should grant tax credits for real estate development for the development or residential property. By granting tax credits, you will also jumpstart the economy in a big way. The tax credits will be applied toward the hiring of former welfare recipients to work as construction workers. The amount of the tax credit should be established by government. The welfare recipients must show their Medicaid card as proof in order for the real estate developer to qualify for tax credits. Since this will be a loss in tax revenues for government, the government should get out of the slumlord business.

How can government get out of the slumlord business? Sell the residential properties to real estate developers. By selling those properties, the government will receive revenue to recover from losses due to granting tax credits during any given fiscal year. Families living in a buildings that were abandoned by landlords will pay the same amount of rent as they paid before. A maintenance fee will be added to the monthly rent.

The real estate developers will get their return on their investment during a period of time. Housing units will become co-ops and each building will have a co-op board. Employees working for the Housing Department will be working for the real estate developers.

Americans will also benefit by having affordable health care for all. When every American have medical coverage, we are able to sleep a lot easier. I will have more details on my health care plan in my next book. We must assume personal responsibility, not only for ourselves and our families but for our neighbors and our nation. The challenge facing us right now is the fight of economic and social justice.

We as a people want economic equality and an economic system that is fair for all Americans. We want to stop corporations from the constant downsizing by laiding off thousands of Americans. The President and Congress should create more enterprise zones. The enterprise zones will create more jobs by creating more small businesses. Tax breaks will be given to more new entrepreneurs because the new entrepreneurs will create jobs by hiring people living in the enterprise zones.

We also must create diversity in the workplace by keeping the current Affirmative Action laws enacted. The United States is the melting pot of the world and our government must set the example. We must participate in local and national elections as voters. We must attend local community board meetings so that we can express our opinions. You may also contact the President of the United States. The President is always interested in hearing from the American people. Remember, the President works for the people, not for the political machine. You may also contact the governor in your home state and you may contact the mayor or town supervisor in your city or town.

All across America, we must Get Up! Stand Up! Stand Up for Your Rights. Get Up! Stand Up! Don't Give Up the Fight. Keep Hope Alive.

What can we do as average Americans to get involved? Contact your local representative in Congress. Let them know, you are interested in seeing this new initiative take place. Form a political action committee (PAC) and join with other lobbyists to push for reforms. Write letters to the editors of newspapers about this issue. By all means, schedule a meeting with a member of Congress and a subcommittee on issues related to housing and labor.

In order to do this, find out from the Congressional Record for a list of scheduled meetings. It is up to you to put pressure on the politicians.

I hope you found these solutions very helpful in your quest for positive change. This book will give you the basic understanding of economics. Knowledge is power and this book will empower you to change your life. Keep the faith.

ABOUT THE AUTHOR

Having been encouraged by friends and community activists to share his experiences and knowledge with others in a book, Michael A. George accepted the call from Michael Vilkin to write The Truth About American Economics. Born in New York City, George currently makes his home in Queens, New York. With an Associate in Applied Science Degree from Orange County Community College and a Bachelor In Science Degree from York College (CUNY), George have aspirations to become an independent publisher.

In addition to the time he devotes to being a member of Black Women In Publishing in New York City and a community volunteer, George also enjoys football, weight lifting, tennis, reading, writing, golf and giving motivational speeches.

SUGGESTIONS FOR FURTHER READING

Economic Literacy by Jacob De Roy. 1995 by Crown Trade Paperbacks

Introduction to Business by Anthony F. McGann. 1979 by John Wiley & Sons, Inc.

Principles of Microeconomic by E. Dwin Mansfield. 1974 by W.W. Norton & Company, Inc.

Elements of Political Economy by James Mill. 1965 by Augustus M. Kelley. Reprints of Economic Classics.

Economics by Paul A. Samuelson & William D. Nordhaus. 1992 by McGraw-Hill, Inc.

Economics: A Self-Teaching Guide by Stephen L. Slavin. 1988 by John Wiley & Sons, Inc.

The Economy Today by Bradley R. Schiller. 1980 by McGraw-Hill, Inc.

What's Wrong With Economics? by Benjamin Ward. 1972 by Basic Books, Inc.

Economics In Plain English by Leonard Silk. 1978, 1986 by Simon & Schuster, Inc.

The Economist Magazine.

Entrepreneur Magazine.

Success Magazine.

INDEX

To order additional copies of **The Truth About American Economics**, complete the information below.

Ship to: (please print)

Name _____

Address _____

City, State, Zip _____

Day phone _____

_____ copies of *The Truth About American Economics*

@ $9.95 each $ _____

Postage and handling @ $** per book $ _____

*** residents add **% tax $ _____

Total amount enclosed $ _____

*Make checks payable to **MAG Publishing***

Send to: MAG Publishing
1120 Ave. of the Americas, Suite 1061 • New York, NY 10036
718-723-5805

To order additional copies of **The Truth About American Economics**, complete the information below.

Ship to: (please print)

Name _____

Address _____

City, State, Zip _____

Day phone _____

_____ copies of *The Truth About American Economics*

@ $9.95 each $ _____

Postage and handling @ $** per book $ _____

*** residents add **% tax $ _____

Total amount enclosed $ _____

*Make checks payable to **MAG Publishing***

Send to: MAG Publishing
1120 Ave. of the Americas, Suite 1061 • New York, NY 1003
718-723-5805